Table of Contents

While every precaution has been taken in the preparation of this book, the publisher assumes no responsibility for errors or omissions, or for damages resulting from the use of the information contained herein.

SPOKEN SILENCE

First edition. October 31, 2017.

Copyright © 2017 L. Isijola.

Written by L. Isijola.

For madre, anywhere you are, is home.

TIME

Bliss it be

Immune to such trivialities of humanity's fallen state
Wonder if they too wonder about our present mortal body
Just as sure as when the woman took the bait
A bite,
Like gravity down came humanity
Angels knew then as they know now
The collapse from celestial to mortal
Brought by the wrinkles in time
Once wrapped in celestial bodies
Now given to decay
Or they may be wholly oblivious
Wrinkle free and floating high unaware of gravity
No menace of crows feet around their eyes
No indelible lines of joy around the lips
No harrowing furrors between their brows from existence

Ancient Minds

My grandmother knows how to do math better than me
While i'm fidling around with digits on the calculator
She pulls out her pen and paper and begins
To construct tidy columns of numbers
Neatly arranged one underneath the other
Carrying one's to add to two's in her head
Drawing a line directly underneath the number tower
A brick wall set on smooth foundation
My clumsy little hands fumble and push the wrong button
Now, to start over

OBSIDIAN

The Wrongness of Black

Because your ebony scares me
I flee
Onyx skin glaring against the noon-day sun
I run
Because I don't understand the extent of layers kin to tar with no relief
Or reprieve of a softer shade
I turn away
Is it wrong to not understand?
Is it wrong to turn?
And run at something that is the opposite of me?
Is it wrong that I become ashamed at something I am not?
Acting on the basis of superiority in this complex color-woven world
Light-bright, I understand, I see from a distance
Dark-night, much harder, must come closer
Breaching the barrier I have been trained to create
Will I ever know what exactly is wrong with your blackness – and why?
I've been taught to breed this belief
To procreate progenies and perpetuate perceptions based on outlines of
a Shade I can never see
Even underneath the brightest light of a thousand suns – it only gets
darker

L. Isijola

Whole

Only the halves are must haves
Must be, half dark continent born
Half white consonants raised
Congolese – Czech blood
Zambia – Moldovan hair
Cameroon – Belarus nose
Namibian – Hungary lips
And you, are too whole
To be a must have

I See You

A tuck here, a nip there but I can still see your Africa
A shade here, a lift there, but its still all over
More length hair, skin bright clear, it's flowing through you
How can you get away?
Your ancestors weren't Grecian neither are you
Chiseling it in and cutting it out will not remove what you are
Africa – its written all over you
The indelible mark of the Sahara
Arched branches of the Baobab
Like the three tribed marks on my grandmother's wrists
Its all over you
How can you get away?
The Greeks had their day,
The Romans had their way but your Africa still stands
Longer than the Nile,
Deeper than the Serengeti
Broader than the bridge separating your nasal septum
Greater than stacked stones that form epic triangles in Alexandria
Your Africa courses through your veins
Wells up 'neath your dermis
Bursting through your pores
Glaring-open and exposed for all to see
Only fools would believe that a nip there, a tuck here
Can still the might of a thousand roaring lions

Blackness in Roman Lands

Yours – obtuse, oblong, bulbous
Quite the opposite of a crescendo – flat
More like a master sculptor toying with the idea of abstract art
Allowing the clay fall where ever it may – carefree and un-severe
Perhaps you can join in the beauty club
Alas – just one thing, that skin of yours
Vibrant as it may be under the noonday sun
True Mahogany
Bright ebony but still the opposite of porcelain
Reminder that you will never belong
Never be the ideal the Roman masses hail
Heralded as masterpieces
Placed on pedals as center-pieces
You, the opposite of pristine white driven snow
Muddied, paper-bag brown
Dusty dusk, reddened earth
Perhaps worse yet a brazen black

Eden

Adama,
I love you
So much I made you my first born
From dust of the earth I sculpted you
Antecedent as my modern art
Prized possession and masterpiece – brilliantly beautiful
To blind those who would seek you harm
They call you Adama,
I named you Eden
Out of your belly I brought forth life
Mid-wife to civilizations, mother to the myriad
Lush and lavish I created your garden
fertile and fruitful I made your womb
Stored gold and silver under your dermis
Bronze and copper to course through your veins
Hair of coal, black as raven
Liquid fossils flowing longer than the Nile
Rubies and sapphires inside your chambers
And diamonds for pupils in almond set eyes
Because I love you
Cloaked in coats of many colors
Obsidian, onyx, bronze, mahogany,
Amber, hazel, cocoa and coffee
My promise arc of rainbow brown
Your voice I made to mimic the sparrows
When you open your mouth to sing
The envy of other lungs and the air it swallows
Graced with rhythm and dance
For Joys in mourning of darker days that lay ahead

Bright laughter when the drum beats of war begin
The tap, clap, hop, skip and rolling beads on your hips
Responding in resilience to the rising rupture of sailing ships
Like jealous siblings, they came
Teasing and mocking, pocking and prodding
"Well what do we have here?"
Knocked down, dragged out, the fight began
Lurking predator pouncing on fresh prey
Claws ripped across taut bellies
Flowing blood red rubies – exposed
Intertwining intestines of copper coils – convulse
Esophagus coughing up black gold giving way
To no reprieve
Like a two-faced lover, they came
Cautiously courting and wooing with empty promises
Sweet little nothings – after all they had nothing
And were in search of your many somethings
Jekyl and Hyding, the charade they could no longer
Masquerade in the day
Soon night came and they preyed
Lunging, pulling and tearing
With each thrust, mines plundered
With each thrust, mind fractured
Gone mental selling birthrights
For poisoned stew
With each thrust death laid siege
Planting seeds in barren wombs to produce
Swollen bellies full of empty promises
I Am, not forgotten
Water falling into fertile land again –
Vivid green and lush
Like sparrows you will sing again

Coming home
To my Eden

Home

If I had it to do, to choose again
It would always be you
You trained my taste to long for you
Budding bulbs of flavors tickling my tongue
Once weaned from my mother's breast
Flavors ingrained in the river of my veins
Engraved in the mitochondria of each cell
I know your taste all too well
Sublime slime of green and white pods broken in water
Form a clear, gelatinous drawl in the pot
Like southern gentlemen bidding you good day in the bayou
Slow and easy on a summer's afternoon
Peppered sauces off the Richter scale
Implode my insides like bombs over buildings
Crumbling and tumbling til my exterior breaks down
Eyes lit red reflecting the fire within
With droplets streaming down to mingle
With the waterfall that my mouth can no longer contain
Ears roaring loud like steam engines
Nose, the only outlet left for relief
but it too becomes a casualty
Constricted by each prickly little hair set ablaze
This is torture
This is brutal
This is pain
I shouldn't want more
But I do
This is pleasure
Knowing you are forging

Iron within my embers
Silver in my crucible
A gold finery I'll be once you're through
To stand strong with the sternum of steel
Backbone of bronze
Shoulders squared set
Eyes burning like those who've eaten fire
And live to tell the tale

KINGDOM COME

Blur

The days all blur into one
Yesterday's gone
Tomorrow is here
Before you know it, a new day brings a new year
Under the same old sky
That wraps and folds itself around all things
Bellow and echoing, beckoning our day of reckoning.
Kingdom come and wills being done
Whose will, mine or yours?
Some Fathers will their children longevity and happiness
Only to have it stolen and snatched by cruelty and disparity
What's mine is mine
What's yours is yours
The good Lord above watches over us all
Paupers and princes
Wealthy and weary
Minutes and moments
One and gone

Story, Tell

Been in distant lands and ancient seas
Seen kings and queens reign supreme
Heard "Light be"' and how its still beaming
And "In the beginning" still being today
Of monarchs and monks
Princes and patriarchs
Philosophers and preachers
Of Kingdom come
While the wiley ones wield death swords and decay
To profit from power
Mayans making marks
Colliding calligraphy of haunting hieroglyphics
To say I too was here with tales to tell
Don't cave man, me
See these clay-colored walls –
My canvass
See the heavens above –
My easel
The fall of greece, city born and torn
Razed to ruins
Ascension of rome and how it too suffered the same
The opal skinned ones and their towering triangles
Rising in defiance to the scorching sun
Sweat dripping from brows with resolve of legacy
To make their mark
To mark their moment
Or else be lost in the sandy grains of what remains
Yet some today question if earthly or heavenly beings

Built these towering totems to testify of the might that rose from the
east
Witnessed times of rebirth and impressions
Pressing out of the ages dark into marvelous light
Paintings, portraits, and printings revolutionizing civilizations
Souls bared on canvasses
Hearts wretched between pages
Torn amidst reality and fantasy
Cathedrals and courts made new with splashes of color
To envy even the skies above
But of one particular figure
Clearly, stands out among the rest
As humble as a child
Wiser than Solomon himself
Fairer than 10,000 beside
And the day he died
All of heaven cried
"Hosanna!" I heard yesterday
"We Have No King!" I heard the next
Until arms spread wide
Nails ridden
Feet crossed
Nails driven
Execution stake, innocent blood shed
Light cloaked in flesh unmasked
Beaten to be broken
Battered to be bruised,
To be the bridge between darkness and light
Lost and the found
Children and the Father
Between creation and the Creator
And as this Son bowed his head

L. Isijola

The sun gave up the ghost -
This darkest of days
Ushered in
Eternal light
I have seen plenty of tales unfold
Many of them untold
Of the less than and the greater than
The righteous and the damned
Perhaps the greatest lie I have heard
Is that an avatar can gain the world for its soul

Enough

The discipline of a monk I don't have
But I have His grace
The heart of a saint I don't possess
But he still calls me His own
The beauty of a rose is not mine
Yet He calls me beloved
The cunning of a clever mind I have not
Still, He calls me wise
The wealth of an Arab king I can't account
But to Him I'm worth more than gold
The strength of a brute is not my might
Yet soldier, he calls me
This load I cannot carry
But He calls me conqueror
The swiftness of a runner I can't muster
But I have a number in the race
These mountains I can't climb so He tells me
Move them
The oceans I can't swim so He makes me lay down
Beside spring waters
Times I fall and fail
Not quite saint not quite sinner
No monk or minister often times sinister
Still I have His love and He has mine

John the Baptist in Black Leather

John the Baptist preached to me today
In quite peculiar fashion
While screaming fire and brimstone
Sinner that I am and the angry God watching
I was watching the side of his shaved head parted to left
With a chunk of the unshaved side gelled to the right –
Smoothed down and sculpted like ocean breaks
Black leather clad legs appearing and reappearing with every step
While he shouted of the woman with the box
Alabaster and her perfume breaking antics
His black leather clad legs were breaking my concentration
I could not see past the beaded brown bracelet
Bopping up and down
Every time he raised his hand
His wild gesticulations were constantly gesturing me
To his uncollared, cream-colored shirt
That hung slightly off his frame
Fluid and flowing
Uninhibited save for more leather that he wore for a jacket
With more vehemence and vabrado he thundered
On God's saving grace and mercy which I very much needed
Because all I could think of was his brown suede shoes
Shuffling frantically from one end of the stage to the other

Faith

Your faith agitates me
Your fire burns with no regret for sand or storm
Rivaling hell and daring oceans to abate
Wonder where you got that fire from?
If you wrestled with Gabriel himself
Until he lit the wick and started the fire foresting in your heart
Not sure how it all went down
Since I can't have you
Tell me where I can find others like you?

Tired

I want to ask him, "Young man don't you get tired?
Don't you ever get tired of asking the good Lord
Up above about the same things day in and day out?"
"Don't you ever want to say – today I will not pray,
I will not fast, I will just be – still"
Is it not in the stillness that you hear His voice loudest?
Is it not in His whisper that the answer comes clearly?
Like running waters to desert dry lips
When your lips tire, is that not when your soul starts
Believing in His amazing grace when graceless words have stopped
And all you have left is your moans and your groans
And your tears that are left to do the praising
That your lips cannot
The praying
That your tongue cannot
The shouting
That your chords cannot
Young man, do you ever get weary of well doing?
Even when you are not doing well how do you continue?
Expectations on the man of the cloth has never been easy
And never will be
The pulpit and the pew jostle for your all
Never dare you waver
Lest you crash and fall
But young man, don't you ever get tired!
Leaning on his everlasting arms
That hold you and mold you
Push you and pull to his grace
To his love,

Aren't they always enough?
Don't you ever get tired of preaching the good news!
The world needs it now more than ever
Don't you ever get tired of praising his name
The world no longer sees lines between holy and profane

Young man don't you ever cease to seek his face
Seek to kneel even when your knees buckle
Don't cease to lift your hands even if they flail and flounder
And the flag of surrender suddenly looks like a shining star
Think of His saving grace and move onward
Soldier march
In this army your weapon are your words
Wield them wisely –
Remember the young boy with the five smooth stones and a sling
Shoot for the mark set before you and don't you look back
Think of the execution stake and His crimson blood
Think of the miry clay that He pulled you from
Think of salvation and think of grace.
Think of peace and think of love
To be shared with all of His children
Beckoning them back home
Young man don't you ever get tired!
And if you fall may angels catch you
Envelop you with wings descending like doves

L. Isijola

Soul

Force-fed falseness
Belching bellows of bland regurgitated, masticated news
Blues, rhythm and all that is
Is not as it appears
Divided and dour, its all so plastic
But your soul is immortal
Flesh may turn to cinder
Enveloped in cellophane
Walking lines of all profane but your soul is real
So seek truth while it may yet be found
For one day the deception will seem as truth
The wolf like a lamb
Fur covered in cotton-wool
Look closer within its eyes
You can see the piercing evil clutching for your soul
The serpent as gentle as a dove
Believe it not
Though narrow and lowly
If you watch its mouth as it speaks
You can see the two-headed beast
Lurking, echoing and beckoning for your soul
There's a reason you yearn for a home that you do not know
For a leader whose name revered
For a time when time disappears
For a day when justice will truly be just
When peace finally rests on humanity
Like a welcomed blanket during frigid cold nights
A day when lie will no longer be called truth
And truth will no longer be called lie

It's apparent that the final hour approaches
Your soul can feel it too because deep calls to the deep
So your soul is calling for home
Real has been bastardized leaving us all fatherless
Calling on a Father we hope can hear
Hope can see
What His earth has become
What His children have turned into
Against and for all that is not –
Not good
Not right
Not just
Not real
But the longing of your soul is real
Keep seeking, and knocking, and asking
Your soul longs to know really
What is real?

Trinity's Gifting to The Lesser Gods

In the likeness and image of God
Trinity made three – spirit, soul, body
So why do we question our supremacy?
Reject claims of superiority and embrace mediocrity
Free willing to accept wages of minimum worth
When the fire that rages within infuriates our being
Red-orange tongues lapping blue-sky gas
To fuel a blazing inferno
gods, are we not?
Words spoken, light is
To speak to existence what is not and see what was not
Be
Pull ideas and thoughts from
A void of nothingness till something is
Abra cadabra's steroid sibling – miracle
Do we not speak and and see
And peak and see that what we speak is
Until we cease to be?
Breath no more
Bones turned into white-washed tombs of silence
Can we not command the rain to still
And the sun to hide mid-day?
To make shadows of ourselves just for play
Playing with parts that give life or take life at whim
Rightly or wrongly
Justly or not
Do we not rule the winds and the waves
The sky and the sea
All that flies above and all that walks below?

Can we not name the stars in orbit and orbit the stars themselves
Watching galaxies go round the rings on wings of our choosing?
Do we not stoke the embers of our blood till it boils
Stirring revolutions within us?
Crashing cities into cinders
Swiftly razing Rome to its knees
With insidious inceptions of ideas
Thoughts and words
Trinity's gifting to the lesser gods
gods wrapped in the mortality of time
Embalmed in the duality of the celestial and terrestrial
Bound – spirit, soul, body,
The ultimate triumvirate
Are we not gods?

Abba

"Name your god please..."
Hold him or her up to the sky
Young Simba style, name this god of yours
She may be mami-water
Half-scaley, half-fleshly
Seven-armed Shiva multitasking
or juggling your wishes on 70 fingers
Name your god please?
Abba is mine

THE SOUND

Possession

It travels from your brain to your spine
From your spine to your limbs
From your limbs to your fingers
From your fingers to your toes and then all over again
It enters into your ears then travels into your heart
Journeys into your soul
Chords over choruses into cortex
Lyrics over arrangements
Merging and melting into the recesses of the cranium
Clefs and trebles tremble in your temple tickling your vocal chords
Til they give way to the melody echoing
Reverberating inside the levitating lobes
It takes over your countenance turning a frown into a grin
A grin into a smile
A smile into an explosion of laughter
Likewise turning a grin into a frown
A frown into a scowl
A scowl into an explosion of tears
Rushing uncontrollably
A river accelerated
A dam unleashed
Symphony and orchestras rising and falling
Falling and rising into cadences of crevices unseen
Yet the heart sways with every note
Beating with each rhythmic tap and clap
Effortlessly in tune with the tuning of the brain – right side first, left
side next
On and on the beat goes
Until a new melody follows

Unnerving and unmoving
Etched into folds unseen
The melodies of yester-years
Still echoing deeply with each possession

Siren

What sad song can I sing today
What weary blues can I blow into the wind today
What clever lines can I concoct to anchor my sailing soul
Assuage my feigning flesh
What mischief can my fingers trail printing marks adorned with
Lofty thoughts breeding syntax
That self same mind cannot grasp
What will my sound bring today
The clanging of pots and pans
Or the symphony of an orchestra
What chaos will be caused today
What storms will arise today to push me from
Safety and comfort to danger and turmoil
What will it be today

GYPSY

East Side Story

Pilgrimage to the East
Pilgrimage to the concrete jungle
City loaded with talent
Burdened with intentions and inventions
Lugging hopes and dreams on shoulders
Collecting spare change along the way
To destined dreams
The city shows no mercy
The cold winds keep breaking
The snow keeps falling
Home is yonder years away and you came here to stay
In this concrete jungle city of no mercy
No anchor
No family, no belonging
But you'll make one
Start a fire with your ideas and survive
Pitch a tent with your ideals and make camp
Where weary-laden sojourners can find reprieve
For their cold hearts and calloused hands

Gold-Digger

Dear future husband
If we ever hit a rough patch you will not starve
I've learned the fine art of making
A dollar out of a dime
That sounds very romantic does it not?
Truth is I'm sick and tired of being broke and poor
Actually what I mean to say, future husband
Is that you will be a multi-millionaire
Or at the least have several thousands to rub together
So I don't have to romanticize poverty like its
Some grand fantasy
And food as some objective notion
A mere concoction of an abstract thought
An illusion that my brain conjures up
A mirage of the utmost torture
My eyes -
Staring at a full plate of rice, beans and meaty stew
My stomach -
Growls and tongue salivates
Torture is what hunger is
Pain is what poverty is
Nothing to romanticize but to endure
Hoping someday you'll move past it
Like rich people look past homeless bums on the street
And pat their wallets fondly
While counting their stocks, bonds, and portfolios in their heads
There's absolutely nothing romantic in
Hallucinating about food
Walking around the kitchen like a ghost on hollowed ground

Closing and opening the fridge door for the hundredth time
As if on the hundred and one time
Suddenly its bare empty belly
Will be stuffed full – a miracle
Manna from heaven
Dear future husband
Surely you can now understand
Why me asking you to have several thousands to rub together
Is more out of practicality than vanity
I've had poverty and starvation as former lovers
And found them equally unromantic

Esther

Like a trumpet blown on a bone-chilling night
Where nothing is heard except the notes floating up to the stars
And then falling back to earth into the listener's ears
A generation needs to hear
What you have to say
Don't worry that you'll be a copy
The Maker had you on His mind the entire time
Before a speckle of sand hit the darkness
Before sound came from void
Before two drops of hydrogen
And an oxygen combined
Before mama knew papa
The vibrations in your voice are like thumbprints in the atmosphere
The frequency and wavelength your sound generates
Reverberates in the universe
Breaking and entering into souls
A lighthouse in a perfect storm
Your siren song does not take but lends
To safety
To refuge
To home
Ears waiting to hear your speech – speak
Minds eager to bend to the whim and the waves of your words
So share freely
Don't be afraid that its already been said – speak
Don't be afraid that its already been thought – think
In this generation
This moment
For this time

Persuasion

The first one I saw was dapper and debonair
A GQ glossy page come to life
Channeling a wall-street tycoon in an all black suit
Tailored to fit his lithe frame
Breaking the mold cast into type by assuming minds
Apparently from the Orient side that breeds tall men
His walk – confident
Taking long strides as if the the sidewalk
His runway
Dare I say
The crowd parted as he came our way
Asian Moses in a slim-fitted suit-sans staff
The second one fit the mold –
Stout but with an undeniable swagger
Adding imaginary inches
His threads – more 'street' than wall-street
Immaculately matching the maroon-colored beanie to his shirt
Slightly sagging loose fitted jeans
His cool kicks rounded out the look
Lean akin to a brother
More followed
Leaving me wondering how
I was blind to a whole category of beauty
But now I see
On a Sunday
The holiest of days
I became a believer in beauty
Of the eastern persuasion

Robot Girl

Early morning rise an early mourning wake
For the ideas that will not be birthed today
Pages that will not be read today
Solitude that will not be spent today
Thoughts that will not be thought today
Robot girl
Scan in
Break
Lunch
Break
Bathroom
"..and the purpose of your call today?"
"...and how may I help you today?"
"....thank you for calling."
End day
Start day
Robot girl awakened with robot sound
Engine car zoom down freeway lanes
Filled with fellow robot boys and girls
Rank and file
Scan in
Scan out
Bark when the call chimes in
Pavlov's dog paid checked responses
Collar-leashed
Free only for the weekend
Treats half spent in less than 48 hours
Food,
Gasoline and

                    L. Isijola

Clothes
To do it all over again
On mourning day

Wander Lust of the Rolling Stone

Of the rolling stone I be
Gather no moss, no not me
Like lily pads floating in Babylon's garden
Hanging petals swaying in the evening breeze
Dangling roots dancing in a wave of wander
An unsteady tide
Yet steady rise and steady fall
Will move me where they may
I will gather no moss for you
My roots will be firmly planted in unfamiliar terrain
Unanchored by belongings of yesterday's memories
Unchained with chords of sensory maps of side roads and blocks
My bedrock bottom will be granite smooth
No feathery whiskers of greeny moss
I'll move right along on the rolling tide
Like streams flowing down the valley
Navigating to foreign shore
Just to reach the sands
And ask
"Form an arrow where to next?"
Sometimes in sometimes out
But never root downwards climbing upwards
I will not stay and remain to tell tales
Ad nauseum of '92 to 2002
What happened
In this exact spot at this exact same time
The last winter
The last summer
Or the last decade

I'll remain scattered like puzzle pieces
Strewn over varying regions
Continents I've never seen hold my content
My mind traverses on journeys
Beyond time and space lusting for wonders
Luring onward toward the sun
Diamond orb glowing magnet
Drawing my Icarus' wings close till I can soar no more
Sending falling black ashes like raindrops to the earth
And I'll say I've been there and I've done that
Not to brag or to boast but because I was a restless
Child wrestling the sandbox of stagnancy
So I chose to dance where ever my two-left feet could take me
I went
To the ocean depths with all its mysteries
Its width boundless holds my remnants
What I've stored cannot be confined within
Four blocked walls of certainty and rituals

THE END

L. Isijola

Bombs over Boston

Used to be bombs over Baghdad we heard on the news
Now its bombs over Boston that broke all the rules
No tea party Joei de vie only screams of hell on heavenly earth
Hearts rend garments aflame
Crimson red running on asphalt black
Reflecting rays of Saturday's sins
Sunday morning guilt-washed
Temple harlots holding daylight parades
Hermes wings delivering dour messages
Sacrifice sufficed until the next quarter of the year
As certain as taxes filed on death's day

One for 50

In my head I do fear that I will be dead
To my talent
To my dream
Dead to my days
Shrively withered black prune with lines folded into creases of
Tender thoughts
Unspoken silence and unrequited dreams
These Amistad shackle-clad thoughts threatening to sprout wings
Shoulder blades bended
Arched and angled for freedom
I've been allotted a limit of days
Will I squander them?
Like a kid in the penny candy store with a dollar bill
Buying sweets to please my tooth yet
Aching for tangible achievements
Stomach nauseous from suppressed
Stories formed in the mind's eye
What will I say?
In pursuit of the a.m. 9 and the p.m. 5
White picket fence, 2.5 children and a miniature sized dog
The dream I have been programmed to dream
Fantasies controlled remotely by principal beings
Exchanged for true talent
Dreams of security
Of serenity
Covering like Grandma's quilt, familiar and safe
Conformity bred dullness propagated as norm
As normal as the king of the jungle
Locked within a four-square iron bar

As normal as an eagle pecking corn on the ground
While looking up to the sky saying
"One day, i too will fly, one day"
To set sail on a bubble balloon adventure
With helium filled words
Prose of fire igniting carriage-filled thoughts
Floating to the blue beyond

Meanwhile exchanging time for dimes
Glass-filled hour grains forming salty dune of my remains
What will I say in the hereafter
When He asks me what have I done with what He gave
Will I studder, stammer and rattle
Snaking through excuses of economy, family pressure, platform
Excuses tall like fescue on northern lawns
Or will I declare
I turned 1 into 50
The one talent I was given
I went out and invested it in
More time
Souls were my soil
Words were my seeds
And I watered each mind, each heart
With my deeds

UNREQUITED

One

He does not see I, He does not see You
He sees One – the loneliest number fitting two
Fitting three in you, three in me – Trinity
Still one
Earthly math crosses two by three
Makes six
Makes for crowded company
Celestial math makes exponents
One
Raised to the power of three in one is
Still one
In the beginning, He made
One
Took from one heart and made another
Crossed one by the other to get –
One
The same logic took a grain of sand
Measured it in the palm of one hand
Took a drop of water and measured it in the other
Balanced both equally and spun axis to exist
Spinning still

Sunday Morning

A Sunday morning kind of love
No, not the lazy one you're thinking of,
Sleeping in till the morning sun comes up - kind
But the waking up before the Son - kind
We both get up
Knees hit ground
Hold hands
Come together before Him
Humble servants in earnest plea
Pod pieces eternally intertwined
Individual yet united, separate yet whole
Where you begin, I end
I end, you begin
Ad infinitum
I want a Sunday morning kind of love
Craving communion upon rising
Breaking bread with bodies kneaded
Silent sung prayers with tongues twisted in a lilting language
Like thirsty children lapping water from a fountain – just for the sheer
joy of it
A language learned by taste and touch
Budding from the understanding of bodies begging for,
Each cilia on the tips of tongues to raise
An anthem
A chorus
A dance
All praises to the Most High
For the serotonin flooding every cortex
Causing consciousness to convulse from fingers

Tracing outlines on the curvature of dermis
I really can't tie a tie
You'll have to teach me
Like you'll teach me how to make your eggs
Scrambled, how your mama used to make them
Grits with butter and all
You'll teach me to tie a tie
Tie a bow, tie something or another – every Sunday morning
Because you know my memory for things that
Loop-de-loop like bows and knots is just not there
But I'll learn one of these days
Maybe when we're sixty and silver gray
Before heading out
I'll ask you to zip me up
You'll manage to pinch the skin on my back – every single time
We'll smile because its Sunday morning
Ties and bows and zippers
Its our Sunday morning kind of love

Humor

Funny, the ironic kind of humor
How the idea of someone can be much stronger
Than the presence of someone
Is it not that when I don't see you, I want you?
Is it not that when I see you, I wish to not have seen you?
Actually,
Stand still
Face me
Let me take a long, hard look at you
To decide
If you're really worth my wanting
To see
If I really want what I see

Ghost

On how a woman
Should write about a man
She had only imagined
What did I see?
What did you seek?
That made us think we were a possibility
Can count on one hand the conversations
Never needed more than that
But if the moment ever came, we'd talk for hours
From the mundane to cerebral
Spiritual to the superfluous
Ridiculous to the random
And we'd laugh at a whole bunch of nothingness in between
Each thinking to the other what could have been
What would have been
If I had stayed and you had proceeded
If you had chased – a bit harder
And I caved – a bit sooner
What would have been, Creator knows
Perhaps nothing at all
Perhaps you'd have chosen the other all along
Perhaps it is as it should be
You and the other
Me and the future
Bride of tomorrow only certain of the King
Everyone else, a doubt
My cross to bear
Daily, my flesh to kill
Asking, my Lord to deliver

Choice

I can't give you what you don't know
Make your wanting tangible
The music has stopped, the seats taken
None left for you to fill
Yet you're still making the rounds
Duck, Duck....Gone
Tag, you're it
Are we still children in grade school?
Toying with fickle emotions
Always on the fringe of making a decision
But never actually making a decision
You love her, no? Then choose her
I love you
Not in the way you love her
but I love you –
Like a big brother
Like an imaginary best friend
Like an older sister
Like a mother – over-protective
Don't be fooled by my placid demeanor
A thousand roaring waves are churning within
I want to tell you I love you – in all of these ways
Let me
I want to tell you that I'm proud of you
That I'm for you
I want to tell you that it's OK
Marry her
Choose her
Love her

Have eyes for no one else – only her
Looking at me or another will make choosing her more difficult
It doesn't have to be
Be abandoned in your choice
However; know this
A second option I cannot be
No use looking my way
When you've found your first

You

I wanna love you more than I love pancakes with warm 100% pure
maple syrup
Atop melted, fresh-churned butter on a lazy Saturday afternoon
Ooeey, Gooey, mushy love
I wanna love you like a good book on a rainy Sunday evening
Nowhere to go, just the two of us
Cuddled under covers
Body-heat
Rhythmic heart-beat as background music
Tracking with droplets hitting glass window panes
I wanna love you, like chocolate, the Belgium or Swiss kind
Rare indulgence that I have no choice but to savor, right now
Lest its gone too soon
I wanna love you like my favorite dress
Hundred percent cotton, hugging my curves yet giving me enough
Space to move, and breath, and be
I wanna love you, like my gift
Not a day of thought without paper and pen
Screen and keyboard
Words from head to eyes
To heart pulsing through nerves to fingertips
Scribbling internal speech to seen thoughts
I want to love you, like His house, This Temple
The no other place I'd rather be
I want to love you
Like a father dancing with his girl like she's the only one in the room
Like a wiser wife
Reminiscing on the starry-eyed husband of her youth
Even more now with silver hairs and dimmed pupils

With milky way rings obscuring once sparkling irises
I still want to love you
I don't know your name, yet
Can't see your face
Yet to examine your frame
But even now, I'll love you, like I know you

The imaginary Heart Ache

I saw her face
A sand castle construction
The imaginary visions and daydreams
Of our togetherness washed away
A child brought my castle down
Her innocent face
Wave hitting shore
Her eyes erased three hundred and sixty-five days of grainy memory
Is that when my body-double entered?
High yellow to my ebony hue
Stepping in on cue
Upon my exit
She's playing the role well
I must say
Mega-watt smile turned on
By your every gaze in her direction
When I thought you were looking at me
You were looking for her
Perhaps she'd always been there
Lurking in my shadow, somewhere over my shoulder
Crossed-signal with no guard
Leaves wounded scars
Where no bandage can reach
I'll remember to get out of the clouds
To see the signs next time
But daydreamer that I am
At it again
Head in clouds imagining your offsprings
Your sienna-brown melting with her sunflower-butter yellow

Molding toffee colored babies
Some butterscotch sweet kids they'll be

Spark

Somewhere among these seven billion hearts
Intellects and emotions and wills
You're roaming, wander-lustily or purposefully
Only you and your maker know
Until we collide
Sparks of nova
Blessing the lucky ones
Til then, I AM,
Arranges the spheres so showers of flaming stars
Can fall like rain until our frail frames
Cease to spark past the hereafter
Prayers to Elohim
In Him, find me

Don't miss out!

Click the button below and you can sign up to receive emails whenever L. Isijola publishes a new book. There's no charge and no obligation.

https://books2read.com/r/B-A-PZCF-HIUP

About the Author

Lola Isijola is a Nigerian-born American poet and novelist based in the Mid-west. She uses poetry to describe the immigrant narrative in America through the female lense. Lola is currently working on her debut novel, Brothers.

Read more at spokensilencepoetry.com.

www.ingramcontent.com/pod-product-compliance
Lightning Source LLC
Chambersburg PA
CBHW030827060726

47590CB00004B/1437